Juneteenth

THIS EDITION
Editorial Management by Oriel Square
Produced for DK by WonderLab Group LLC
Jennifer Emmett, Erica Green, Kate Hale, *Founders*

Editor Maya Myers; **Photography Editor** Nicole DiMella; **Managing Editor** Rachel Houghton;
Designers Project Design Company; **Researcher** Michelle Harris;
Copy Editor Lori Merritt; **Indexer** Connie Binder; **Proofreader** Susan K. Hom;
Sensitivity Reader Ebonye Gussine Wilkins; **Series Reading Specialist** Dr. Jennifer Albro

First American Edition, 2024
Published in the United States by DK Publishing, a division of Penguin Random House LLC
1745 Broadway, 20th Floor, New York, NY 10019

A catalog record for this book is available from the Library of Congress.
HC ISBN: 978-0-7440-9440-4
PB ISBN: 978-0-7440-9439-8

DK books are available at special discounts when purchased in bulk for sales promotions, premiums, fund-raising,
or educational use. For details, contact:
DK Publishing Special Markets, 1745 Broadway, 20th Floor, New York, NY 10019
SpecialSales@dk.com

Printed and bound in China

The publisher would like to thank the following for their kind permission to reproduce their images:
a=above; c=center; b=below; l=left; r=right; t=top; b/g=background
Alamy Stock Photo: Bob Daemmrich 21br, Niday Picture Library 19cla, North Wind Picture Archives 13b;
Collection of the Smithsonian National Museum of African American History and Culture: Gift of the
Scurlock family 3; **DeGolyer Library, Southern Methodist University:** 19t; **Dreamstime.com:** Alexeysmirnov 1,
Matt Antonino 27bl, Michael Gray 27cb, Kunnapat Jitjumsri 27tr, Caroline Klapper 27br, Trong Nguyen 11b,
Daniel Thornberg 12t, Vadimrysev 25crb; **Getty Images:** Anadolu 4-5, API / Gamma-Rapho 11c, Archive Photos /
MPI / Stringer 22cla, Denver Post / Kathryn Scott Osler 6-7, Hearst Newspapers / Houston Chronicle /
Karen Warren 18b, Jose Luis Pelaez Inc 26b, MediaNews Group / Orange County Register 28-29, Stringer /
Jon Cherry 30b; **Library of Congress, Washington, D.C.:** Gen. Gordon Granger 17tl, George Harper Houghton
9tr, Kurz & Allison-Art Publishers, 76 & 78 Wabash Ave., 14t, LC-USZ62-133069 16b, Russell Lee 20, Warren K
Leffler 23b, Henry P Moore 10b, Negro slaves Edisto Island, S.C. plantation of James Hopkinson. South Carolina
Edisto Island, 1862. 9b, United States slave trade. Pennsylvania Washington, D.C. Philadelphia, 1830. 8t;
U.S. government works: 15, 24-25; **Courtesy of U.S. Army:** Spc. Matthew Marcellus 6br;
Wikimedia Commons: On this Day / US Government 16cr

Cover images: *Front:* **Library of Congress, Washington, D.C.:** (Background); **Shutterstock.com:** Roman
Samborskyi c; *Back:* **Getty Images / iStock:** DigitalVision Vectors / diane555 cra, clb

All other images © Dorling Kindersley
For more information see: www.dkimages.com

www.dk.com

MIX
Paper | Supporting
responsible forestry
FSC™ C018179

This book was made with Forest
Stewardship Council™ certified
paper – one small step in DK's
commitment to a sustainable future.
Learn more at
www.dk.com/uk/information/sustainability

Juneteenth

Sarah Fuentes

Contents

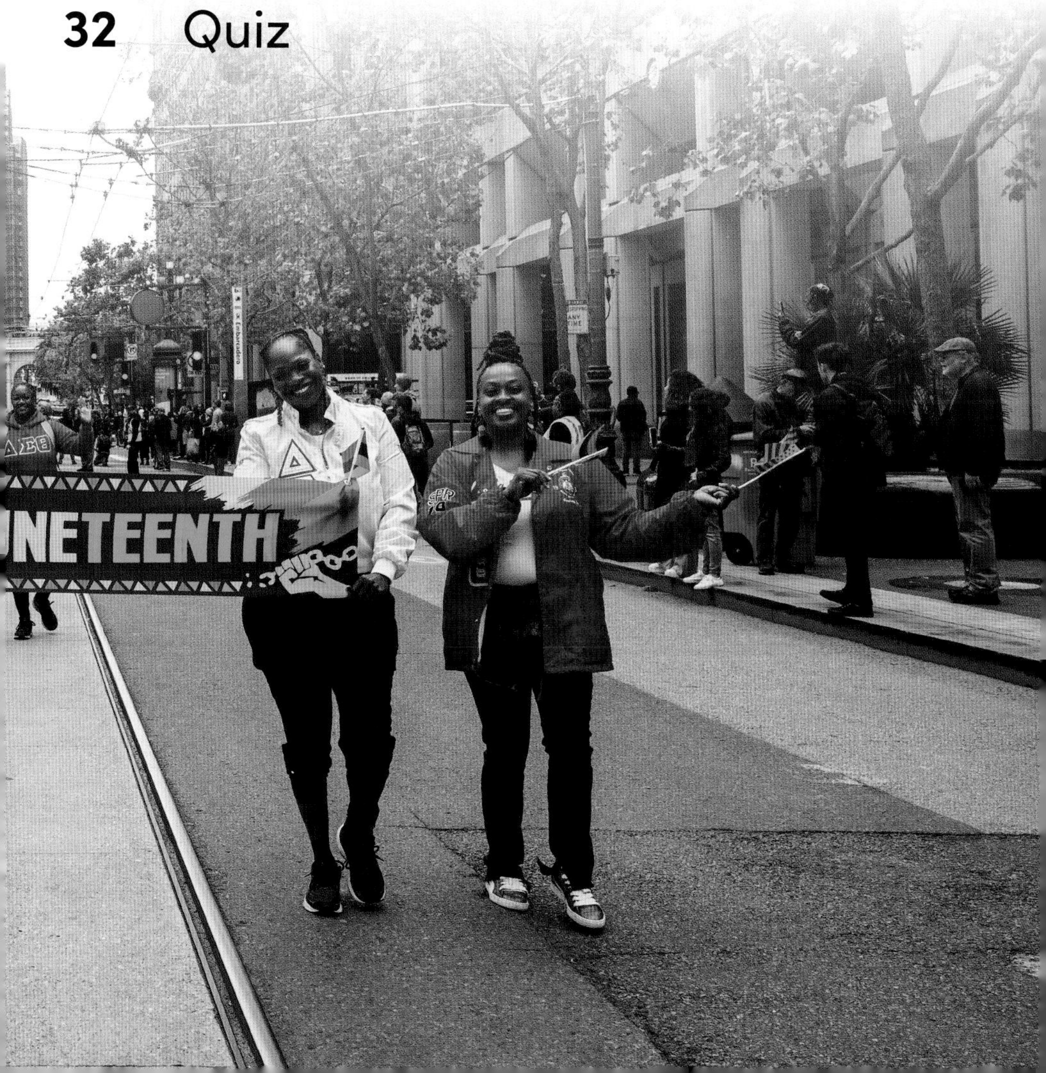
NETEENTH

What Is Juneteenth?

Juneteenth is a national holiday. It celebrates June 19, 1865. This was the day when enslaved Black people in Texas found out they were free.

The name Juneteenth is a combination of **June** and nine**teenth**. It started as an African American celebration in Texas. Today, it is a national celebration of freedom.

UNITED STATES SLAVE TRADE.
1850.

Slavery in America

Slavery was legal in America from the early 17th century until 1865. Millions of people were kidnapped from their homes in Africa. They were taken across the ocean in chains. In America, people could buy and own Africans. The owners forced the Africans to do hard work for no pay for their whole lives. This was called slavery.

Enslaved people had no personal rights. They had no freedom. Their owners could treat them any way they wanted.

Many enslaved people tried to fight back or run away. But if they were caught, they were punished harshly.

Enslaved Africans had difficult lives. They were punished for not following rules. They were beaten for not working hard enough.

Many of them worked in the fields of large farms. These farms were called plantations. They grew crops like tobacco, cotton, and sugarcane. They had to grow as many crops as possible.

The more crops they grew, the more their owners could sell.

Children were enslaved, too. Enslaved children did not go to school. They worked.

Families Torn Apart

Sometimes, families could not stay together. Parents and children could be sold to different owners. This made life even harder.

Americans fought for freedom from Great Britain in the Revolutionary War. The Declaration of Independence was announced on July 4, 1776. Many Americans celebrated Independence Day. They were free from Great Britain's rule. But enslaved African Americans were not yet free. Slavery continued for nearly 90 more years.

In the northern states, many people believed slavery was wrong. They fought to end it. Many people in the southern states wanted to keep slavery. Plantation owners sold the crops grown by enslaved people. They made a lot of money doing this.

The disagreement over slavery was the main reason for the Civil War. Eleven southern states broke away from the United States. They formed the Confederacy in 1861. The Civil War was fought between the United States and the Confederacy.

President Abraham Lincoln wanted the war to end. On January 1, 1863, he signed the Emancipation Proclamation. This said that enslaved people in the Confederacy were free. This was a major step toward ending slavery. But it was not the end.

President Barack Obama showing guests a copy of the Emancipation Proclamation hanging in his office at the White House, 2010

June 19, 1865

Many enslaved people were not told about the Emancipation Proclamation. It took more than two years for the news to reach all enslaved people.

The Civil War ended in the spring of 1865. On June 19, 1865, Major General Gordon Granger went to Galveston, Texas. In Texas, 250,000 people were still enslaved. Granger announced General Order Number 3. It told people about the Emancipation Proclamation. The enslaved people in Texas finally learned that they had been freed. People around the country celebrated this news.

Jubilee Day

One year later on June 19, African Americans in Texas had a celebration. They called the day Jubilee Day. They dressed up in new clothes. They read the Emancipation Proclamation out loud. They held prayer meetings and sang spirituals.

Emancipation Park, in Houston, Texas, created in 1872 to honor Jubilee Day

People gathered at churches and parks. They had parades, cookouts, and picnics. They competed in rodeos, baseball games, and pageants. They made displays of great things African Americans had done.

In the 1890s, the name of the celebration changed to Juneteenth.

Continued Struggle

Many years passed. African Americans were no longer enslaved, but life was still hard for them. In the South, unfair laws treated Black and white people differently. Laws kept people separate because of their race. People also celebrated Juneteenth to protest unfair laws.

Voting Rights

African American men had the right to vote starting in 1870, but some rules made it very hard for them to do so. On Jubilee Day, politicians helped people learn about their voting rights.

REGISTER TO VOTE HERE

REGISTR
A VOT

Spreading the Celebration

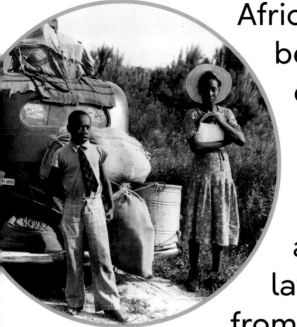

African Americans began moving out of the South. They wanted better jobs and fairer laws. People from Texas brought Juneteenth traditions to other parts of the country.

During the 1950s and 1960s, African Americans fought hard for civil rights. Juneteenth celebrations became more popular.

In 1980, Texas became the first state to recognize Juneteenth as a holiday.

After that, celebrations grew larger each year.

Juneteenth Today

In the summer of 2020, people protested for the rights of African Americans. Juneteenth celebrations spread across America. More people learned about Juneteenth. They learned why it is important to American history.

On June 17, 2021, Juneteenth became a holiday for the whole country.

President Joseph R. Biden signing a bill to make Juneteenth a federal holiday

A Flag for Juneteenth

In 1997, Ben Haith and Lisa Jeanne Graf designed a flag for Juneteenth. They used the colors of the US flag: red, white, and blue. The white star represents freedom. The arc represents a new beginning and hope for the future.

Juneteenth Eats

Food is an important part of any celebration. On Juneteenth, people eat barbecue and soul food. African Americans remember their African roots by drinking sweet hibiscus tea. Hibiscus is a red flower native to West Africa. People eat lots of red foods on Juneteenth.

Strawberry Soda

Enslaved people were not allowed to drink strawberry soda. Today, people drink strawberry soda on Juneteenth because they are free to drink anything they want.

They eat red velvet cake, red beans and rice, hot sauce, and red fruits. Red foods remind us of the struggle of enslaved people. They remind us of the ways they fought back.

Let's Celebrate!

Everyone deserves to be free. Everyone deserves to be treated fairly. On Juneteenth, we remember the importance of treating everyone with kindness. We honor the great things African Americans have done for our country.

On Juneteenth, people of all backgrounds can come together to celebrate freedom, equality, and respect.

Juneteenth is more than an African American celebration. Juneteenth is a chance for all Americans to appreciate the importance of freedom.

Glossary

Civil rights
Rights that promise equal opportunities and fair treatment for all people regardless of their race, sex, gender, religion, or nationality

Crops
Things grown on a farm or plantation to be sold

Emancipation
The act of making people free

Emancipation Proclamation
A document issued by Abraham Lincoln that freed enslaved people in the Confederacy

Enslaved
Living in slavery, forced to work without pay

Equality
Treatment that is the same for all people

Freedom
The ability to choose how you live

Independence
Freedom from rule by another person or government

Plantation
A large farm that depended on enslaved people to do much of the work

Protest
To act, speak, or march in order to change something considered to be wrong

Register
To sign up to do something, like voting

Slavery
The practice of owning people and forcing them to work without pay

Spiritual
A song that has religious or emotional meaning. Spirituals were created by Black people in the US during the time of slavery to give them hope for a better future.

Index

Quiz

Answer the questions to see what you have learned. Check your answers in the key below.

1. What does Juneteenth celebrate?

2. What was the original name for Juneteenth?

3. Where and when were the last enslaved people told about the Emancipation Proclamation?

4. What color are many of the foods eaten on Junetenth?

5. What year did Juneteenth become a federal holiday?

1. Freedom 2. Jubilee Day 3. Galveston, Texas, on June 19, 1865
4. Red 5. 2021